How to Wait for A Godly Mate

Cherry Woods

authorHOUSE®

AuthorHouse™
1663 Liberty Drive
Bloomington, IN 47403
www.authorhouse.com
Phone: 1-800-839-8640

First published by AuthorHouse   4/6/2011

ISBN: 978-1-4567-5258-3 (e)
ISBN: 978-1-4567-4766-4 (sc)

Library of Congress Control Number: 2011903764

Printed in the United States of America

Any people depicted in stock imagery provided by Thinkstock are models, and such images are being used for illustrative purposes only. Certain stock imagery © Thinkstock.

This book is printed on acid-free paper.

How to Wait
for A Godly Mate

Cherry Woods

authorHOUSE®

AuthorHouse™
1663 Liberty Drive
Bloomington, IN 47403
www.authorhouse.com
Phone: 1-800-839-8640

First published by AuthorHouse   4/6/2011

ISBN: 978-1-4567-5258-3 (e)
ISBN: 978-1-4567-4766-4 (sc)

Library of Congress Control Number: 2011903764

Printed in the United States of America

Any people depicted in stock imagery provided by Thinkstock are models, and such images are being used for illustrative purposes only. Certain stock imagery © Thinkstock.

This book is printed on acid-free paper.

Dedication

To my Lord and Savior Jesus Christ who paid my sin debt in full, and whose unconditional love has sustained me all of my life.

To my precious and loving daughter Anitra Woods who has always been my greatest fan. Thanks so much for encouraging me to stir up the gifts that God has entrusted me with. You are a precious jewel and I thank God every day for the privilege of being your mother.

To my mother, Missionary Mariah Matthews who taught me from an early age that, "with God all things are possible."

Contents

Preface

In the last decade God has allowed his daughter's to accomplish great things. He has positioned us in new ministries, homes, cars, businesses, and careers. We have learned how to achieve success in the boardroom, and the classroom. We have the luxury car, the condo, the Master's Degree, and the corner office. But somehow we continue to experience failure after failure in our love lives. For some reason, that godly husband that we desire never seems to find us. I mean that truly saved, born-again, washed in the Blood, Holy Ghost filled, and fire baptized man of God. A man who will lay on his face before God, until he hears from heaven, a man who is totally in love with God so that you can be confident in his love. Not a perfect man, but a praying man.

Have you ever cut into a cake and found that the center was not done? The cake appeared to be ready; it had been cooled and frosted. The fragrance of freshly baked cake wafted all through the house. It looked absolutely delectable, and you just had to cut one small slice before dinner. But once the knife hit center; you discovered that the cake was not ready. Some of us have the same problem; we appear to be together on the outside, but our inside is in need of major repair. We may be nursing old hurts, battling low self-esteem, harboring unforgiveness, or lacking self-control in our spending. But there is good news; God is willing and able to heal every hurt, and to give us the wisdom we need to overcome every issue in our lives. After, and only after; we are truly prepared for our mates; will God allow them to enter our lives.

The purpose of this book is to help godly women to prepare for their mates while receiving the healing that they need. As children of God we expect his best, and in order to receive his best sons; we need to become his best daughters. My sisters I pray that you are blessed by the words on these pages; and that you will find some wisdom in them. I pray even more that you find healing to the depths of your being; as you escape the prison of the past and realize how awesome you really are. The journey that you are about to take with me will help to prepare you for your mate; from the inside out. Sit back and relax; God is in control!

One
Do You Love Him?

For God so loved the world, that he gave his only
begotten Son that whosoever believeth in him should
not perish, but have everlasting life.
John 3:16 (KJV)

The desire to be loved is in our nature, and was placed there by God himself. From the moment we are born we show our desire to be loved by crying for our mothers to hold us in their arms. Our need for human contact; and words of love and comfort continue throughout our lives. However, as Christian women, we must allow God to prepare us for marriage by teaching us how to give and to receive love. First, we must learn to love the one who loves us most of all; our Heavenly Father. It is easy to say that we love God, but do our actions reflect that love? Do we obey him at all times without hesitation? Do we spend quality time with him? How faithful are we in keeping the promises that we make to Him? Do we reverence him as he has commanded us? If you have answered no to any of these questions it is time to check your love thermometer. It is either stuck or broken; in either case it is malfunctioning. The cure for a malfunctioning love thermometer requires prayer, fasting, and a daily diet of God's Word. Unlike most cures this one is guaranteed to work, and will restore our passion, love and fear of God. We will also rediscover how much the Lord truly loves us and desires to spend time with us. Developing a loving relationship with the Father is the first step in learning to love both ourselves and others.

We build successful relationships by learning about the other person's interests, likes and dislikes. This requires spending quality time with them and not only talking with, but listening to them as well. Building a relationship with the Father requires the same type of dedication. We learn about the Lord from reading his Word and meditating on it. Merely picking up the Bible and reading a few verses of scripture does not constitute meditating on the word. Meditate means, "to focus one's thoughts on: reflect on or ponder over." Therefore, meditating on scripture means to think deeply about the words we are reading, and to seek to understand them. In doing so, we begin to know God in a deeper way and also prove our commitment to Him and to his Word.

The Word of God declares, "But his delight is in the law of the Lord; and in his law doth he meditate day and night. And he shall be like a tree planted by the rivers of water, that bringeth forth his fruit in his season; his leaf also shall not wither, and whatsoever he doeth shall prosper" (Psalm 1: 2-3 [KJV]).According to the scripture when we meditate on the Word of God, it pleases him so much that he blesses us. The scripture says that whatever we do will prosper and we shall bring forth fruit in our season. This means that God will bless everything that we put our hands to, and that we will stand firm and undefeated. As we seek to understand his word, the closer we become to him. The word of God tells us in James 4:8 (KJV), "Draw nigh unto God, and he will draw nigh unto you."

God's word is our roadmap; it is the Christian instruction manual. The Bible says, "Thy word is a light unto my feet, and a lamp unto my path." (Psalm 119:105 [KJV]). This means that if we spend time in God's word; he will lead and guide us in every area of our lives. If we allow his word to guide and illuminate our footsteps, we will not take the wrong path, make the wrong decisions, or choose the wrong mate! That is why it is so important to feast on the word of God daily. Every day of our lives we have to make some type of decision, if we have the word of God down in hearts it will help us to make the right choice every time. Make the Word a part of your "spiritual diet" by spending

3

time in it daily. Being the faithful woman of God that you are, you probably attend Sunday school and mid-week Bible study every week; however, you still need to spend time in the word each day. You feed your body 7 days a week, and it is equally important to do the same for your spirit! Think about how malnourished your body would become if you only ate two meals a week. The same thing happens to your spirit when you fail to spend enough time in the word of God. Your spirit becomes weak and vulnerable to the enemy's deception and to sin.

If you find it difficult to spend time in the word daily due to a hectic schedule, get up thirty minutes earlier and spend time meditating on a few verses of scripture. Soon you will begin to develop an even greater hunger for the word of God, and find yourself rising even earlier in order to spend more time in his word. That's the way love is; the more time you spend with someone who loves you, the more you begin to love them and the stronger the relationship grows. God not only created love, he *is* love, and if we cannot commit to spending time with him, and loving him with our entire being; how can we commit to loving an individual for a lifetime? How can we spend 4 hours going to dinner and a movie with someone that we do not know, and may not even *like* once we do; and then be incapable of spending thirty minutes a day getting to know the one who gave all for us? Do you remember who healed your broken heart the last time that you gave it to the wrong person? *God!* Always faithful, always steadfast, *God!*

Developing a close relationship with the Father requires that we spend time in prayer. We must learn to spend time in prayer not only when we need or want something from God; but because we love him and desire his presence. Prayer is not just talking to God, but also listening to what he has to say. If you sincerely desire to just rest in the Lord's presence and let him minister to you, just kneel to him and open up your spirit. He will draw more closely to you than you could have ever imagined, you will sense his presence like never before. He will renew and refresh your spirit as you submit to him completely. He will show you great and mighty things, and he will assure you that not only has he heard your prayers, he has answered them. He was just waiting for you to stop talking and start listening.

God wants us to spend quality time with him. He is interested in everything that concerns us, and wants us to have his best. However, he wants us to give him our best as well. He is our Father and creator and he must always come first in our lives. The word of God states, "And thou shalt love the Lord thy God with all thine heart, and with all thy soul, and with all thy might" (Deuteronomy 6:5 [KJV]). This is not a suggestion, but a commandment from God, and if we desire his blessings we must obey him. Each of us has been guilty of putting our wants before God in some area in our lives, so let us go before the throne of grace and ask his forgiveness.

Father in the Name of Jesus, I confess that I have been guilty of putting my desires before yours. I ask that you forgive me for failing to love you with all of my heart, soul, and might. I ask that you teach me how to avoid making this mistake again. From this day forward I commit to spending time in your word and in prayer each day, so that I might come to know you more intimately. It is my desire to discover your perfect will for my life, in the Mighty Name of Jesus, Amen.

God also requires that we learn to trust in him completely. When we learn to trust God in every situation, our faith increases which draws us into a closer relationship with him. The Bible says, " But without faith it is impossible to please him, for he that cometh to God must believe that he is, and that he is a rewarder of them that diligently seek him" (Hebrews ll:6[KJV]). The word *trust* is defined as, "assured reliance on the character, ability, strength, or truth of someone or something." As believers we know that God can neither lie nor fail, and that no one's character measures up to his. We can believe his truth and trust in his strength when everyone and everything else fails. When our families, finances, relationships, health, ministries and careers seem to be falling apart, God remains faithful, consistent, and trustworthy. It is he who keeps us from losing hope, and sometimes our lives in times of trouble. We seem to trust in so many things that are fallible in our lives. How many times do you sit in the chair at your desk without considering the possibility that it may fail to support you? You just assume that since it has never fallen apart, there is no cause for concern. Well, what about God? When has he ever let us down, left us alone, failed, or lied to us? Who or what is more reliable or more dependable than he is? No one! The Bible proclaims, "Trust in the Lord with all thine heart, and lean not unto thine own understanding. In all thy ways acknowledge him, and he shall direct thy paths" (Proverbs 3:5-6 [KJV]). Failing to trust God causes us to become involved in relationships with the wrong person, which sets us up for certain heartache. Thank God for his grace, mercy and willingness to forgive. Let's recommit to trusting in him, by saying the prayer below:

Father in the Name of Jesus, I ask that you forgive me for my lack of trust in you. I know that you love me with an everlasting love, and that you will never leave or forsake me. Teach me to trust you in every area of my life, in Jesus Name, Amen.

God expects us to invest time in service to our local church and to our community. It does not matter if you cannot sing, preach, or teach Sunday school, each of us have the ability to serve in some capacity. God has given each of us some type of gift; whether it is baking, organizing events, decorating, or some other talent. While we wait for God to send us the mate that we desire, we need to prepare ourselves by learning how to serve. If you have a problem with serving others, you may be better off single. Marriage is a ministry of love, devotion, *and service* to your spouse.

Sometimes finding the time to serve in our local church can seem overwhelming; especially to the career woman that is also a full-time student; or the single mom that works a second job. But be encouraged; God does not expect you to serve on every church committee, the usher board, sing with the praise team and the choir, and work with the Youth Department. He knows that we must have balance in order to retain good mental and physical health. Find out where help is needed in your church, and then seek the Lord's guidance in where he wants you to serve. Wherever you are called to serve, do it whole heartedly. The Bible says, "And whatsoever you do, do it heartily, as to the Lord and not unto man" (Colossians 3:23 [KJV]).

As Christians we should spend time serving in our communities in some way. Every day God gives us the opportunity to bless someone in word or deed. We are not all available to work with a community organization, or local charity, but each of us can contribute in some way. God has *commanded*, "Thou shalt love thy neighbor as thyself" (Mark

12: 31 [KJV]). The only commandment which is greater than this, is to love God with all of your being (Mark 12: 30). There are people in our neighborhoods, churches, and in our workplaces struggling to make ends meet everyday. There are elderly people who are unable to keep their homes properly heated or cooled, because their Social Security is not quite enough. Some of them are reduced to eating very little or nothing at all; while some of us throw away more food than the elderly are able to buy each month.

There are ways that we can help others in need, if we are willing to put forth a little extra effort. Do you know of someone who may need food, heat, clothing or other everyday necessities? If you don't; ask God to make you more sensitive to the needs of those around you. Some single mother's heart is breaking because her paycheck is not enough to feed her children the entire month. There is a father somewhere who has always worked hard to provide for his family, but has recently lost his job due to cutbacks at his company. You may be facing similar circumstances, but as a child of God you know that when we take our minds off of ourselves we open the door for God to pour out his blessings on us. Hosting a benefit, church or community yard sale, bake sale or food drive, and employing the help of the women in your church or community can help to relieve the suffering of those in need As the word of God says, "Be not deceived God is not mocked, for whatsoever a man soweth, that shall he also reap."(Galatians 6:7 [KJV]). If you take the time to bless others, you will reap blessings. This is God's promise to you; and he always keeps his word.

As Christians we should perform random acts of kindness. As a matter of fact, if God's spirit really lives in us; showing kindness to others should be second nature. Have you ever stood in line behind someone struggling to scrape up just enough change to pay for their food in the grocery store; and refused to help that person, knowing that the Holy Spirit is compelling you to pay that $1.15? If so, you have either missed the opportunity to bless another Christian, or to witness to an unbeliever by failing to let God use *you* to show his love. You are also in disobedience when you can help someone and refuse to do so. Remember that it is God who allows you to work and earn your wages; and that in an instant you could find yourself in the same situation. Many of us have experienced financial struggles to some extent; and would do well to remember that it was *God* that brought us out. In the end; we will answer to *him* for how we have treated those in need.

Then shall they also answer him saying, Lord when saw we thee an hungered, or athirst, or a stranger, or naked, or sick, or in prison, and did not minister unto thee. Then shall he answer them saying, verily

I say unto you in as much as ye did it not to one of the least of these, ye did it not to me.

Matthew 25:44 (KJV)

This is Jesus speaking; this passage of scripture is written in *red*. Each of us will answer to him for how we have responded to those in need. The bible also says, "Withhold not good from them whom it is due, when it is in the power of thine hand to do it" (Proverbs 3:27 [KJV]). God never asks us to do what we are not able to do. He *knows* exactly how much money we have. However, there are times when he will ask you to sow sacrificially into someone else's life. But don't panic, God is not broke! He tells us in Proverbs 19:17 (KJV), "He that hath pity upon the poor lendeth unto the Lord and that which he hath given will he pay again." He also tells us, "He that giveth to the poor shall not lack; but he that hideth his eyes shall have many a curse" (Proverbs 28:27 [KJV]). Which do you desire for your life; blessing or cursing? The choice is yours.

Father in the Name of Jesus, I come to you asking that you reveal to me where I can be of service in my church and my community. You have blessed me in so many ways that I cannot withhold from those in need any longer. I will obey you as you show me where to serve, and to sow of my time, talents, and blessings. I chose blessing over cursing and prosperity over lack. Forgive me for disobeying you those times that I neglected to give to others when it was in my power to do so. I realize that obedience is more pleasing to you than sacrifice and from this day forward I will obey you in my giving, in Jesus Name, Amen.

Two
The Power Of Forgiveness

And forgive us our debts, as we forgive our debtors.
Matthew 6:12 (KJV)

Like any good father, God knows what is best for his children; and knows when to say yes, no, or *not yet*. In fact he loves us so much, that he will not give us anything that we are not mature enough nor prepared enough to handle. Those of us who are parents know that it is sometimes necessary to say "not yet" to our own children, for their protection. We know what our children can and cannot handle, and we make decisions accordingly. A parent would not buy their child a ten speed bike if they couldn't ride a tricycle, because they could be hurt or even killed just *trying* to ride the bike. And when one of our children is injured, we watch over them carefully until they are healed. The Bible says, "If ye then, being evil, know to give good gifts

13

to your children, how much more shall your Father which is in heaven give good things to them that ask him" (Matthew 7:11 [KJV]).

God is all-knowing; therefore, he is well aware of our ability to handle every situation in our lives. The Lord is not going to send "Boaz" until we have not only learned to love, but also to forgive. The ability to forgive requires spiritual maturity. It is not always easy to forgive, especially when we are hurt by those that are supposed to love and protect us. However, we are commanded by God to forgive those who have caused us pain. The Bible proclaims, "For if you forgive men, when they sin against you, your heavenly Father will also forgive you. But if you do not men their sins, your Father will not forgive your sins" (Matthew 6:14 [NIV]). Unforgiveness impacts the life of the offended more than it does the life of the offender. When we fail to forgive others our spiritual, physical, and mental health is affected. Refusing to forgive not only causes us to walk in disobedience to God, but also hinders the blessings that he desires to pour out on us.

Although God commands us to forgive those who have hurt us, he does not take it lightly when his children are hurt. Luke 17:1 (KJV) says, "Then said he unto the disciples, it is impossible for that offences will come, but woe until him through whom they come." The Bible also states." Dearly beloved, avenge not yourselves, but rather give place unto wrath, for it is written, VENGENCE IS MINE; I WILL REPAY, saith the Lord "(Romans 12:19 [KJV]). God will avenge us when our enemies rise against us. But remember that God is rich in mercy and if our enemies repent, he will forgive them; whether we like it or not. And if God can forgive them, who are we not to do the same?

Forgiveness is a powerful force and brings healing and restoration to us. When we are bound by unforgiveness, we cannot receive the healing that we need. Yes; people can really tear our hearts apart; they can hurt us in ways that we have never imagined. But at some point in our lives we must let go of the pains of the past, and stop allowing the devil to remind us of how badly we were hurt. He is a thief, and if we are saved he cannot steal our souls, but if we give him place, he will steal our joy. Refuse to fall for the enemy's tricks, and renew your mind with God's word. Pick up your bible and begin to meditate on the promises of God, put on some good gospel music and get your praise on, and don't give the devil any place.

When we form new love relationships before our hearts have been completely healed; we either end up choosing the wrong person and getting our hearts broken again, or taking out our hurt and anger on someone who does not deserve it. For instance, if we have not healed from the pain of having an unfaithful spouse, we are likely to view every man as a cheater. We may even become verbally abusive; accusing the new man in our lives of unfounded offences. Waiting until we are free from the pain of past disappointments protects us and others from unnecessary heartache.

Harboring unforgiveness against others robs us of living the abundant life that God has purposed for us. Sadly some of us are still angry with people who are now deceased, or have completely forgotten that we are even alive. How many years have you allowed unforgiveness to steal from you? How many opportunities have you missed to find love? Complete the exercise below by listing the names of those who hurt you in the past and how they hurt you. Next, list how many years have passed since the offence occurred. When you have completed the exercise, calculate the amount of time that you have allowed the enemy to steal from you. Finally go to the Father and confess the sin of unforgiveness; so that he can bring healing and restoration to your life.

Name	Offence	When
1.		
2.		
3.		
4.		
5.		

Father in the Name of Jesus, I confess the sin of unforgiveness and repent sincerely for allowing the enemy to steal days, months, or years from my life. I ask that you heal me everywhere that I hurt today, and restore my joy as only you can do, in Jesus Name. Amen.

Now that you have released everyone else that hurt you in your past, it is time to forgive *yourself.* We often find that is more difficult to forgive ourselves; then it is to forgive others. The sins and mistakes of our pasts often continue to haunt us, even though years have passed. We must not allow the enemy to burden us with guilt over sins that God has forgiven. The precious blood of Jesus washed away all of your sins, guilt and shame; when you gave your life to him.

You may have had an abortion, an affair, or served time in prison, but if you have repented of your sins, then God has not only forgiven them, he no longer remembers them. God does not hold grudges. Nor is he sitting in heaven waiting for you to make a mistake so that he can remind you of the sins of your past. The word of God proclaims, "as far as the east is from the west, so far has he removed our transgressions from us" (Psalm 103:12 [NIV]). When God looks at us, he no longer sees the sins we committed in our past. He sees us as blood washed, born again believers. The word of God also tells us, "For I will be merciful to their unrighteousness, and their sins and their iniquities will I remember

17

no more" (Hebrews 8:12 [KJV]). That means that when you have sincerely repented for your sins, God himself wipes the slate clean! Jesus took your place on the cross; therefore, you are redeemed by his blood. Your sin debt is paid in full. Honor him by letting go of the guilt of your past, and celebrating the new life he has given you. Forgiving yourself brings healing, joy and peace to your life. Don't allow the enemy to steal any more of your time then he already has. Bury the guilt from your past today, and never give yourself permission to exhume it!

Father in the name of Jesus, I lay the guilt of my past at your feet today. I will no longer remind myself of the sins that you have long forgotten. Thank you for sending your Son Jesus Christ to pay my sin debt in full, in His name. Amen.

Three
Learn To Love You

Who satisfieth thy mouth with good things, so that thy
youth is renewed like the eagle's
Psalm 103:5 (KJV)

After building a loving relationship with God, there is one more person you must learn to love unconditionally, and that person is *you*. Most of us believe that we do love ourselves, but our behavior speaks otherwise. We continue to allow unhealthy relationships to develop, often with ungodly men knowing that the end result is certain heartache. Sometimes we think just because a man is saved that he is the one for us, some of us have learned the hard way that this is not always true. Just because he is a saved man doesn't mean he is *your* saved man. The fact that you are both saved does not guarantee that you will be compatible in a love relationship. God may have sent this man into your life to be your friend rather than your mate. If you are not certain, seek God's wisdom. Don't allow loneliness, desperation, or low self-esteem to cause you to continue to make bad choices.

Low self-esteem is the reason that most of us develop, or remain in unhealthy relationships. As daughters of Almighty God we are treasured, cherished, and loved with an everlasting love. We are valuable, precious and beautiful to our Father and must learn to see ourselves the way that he does. However, this can be difficult if we lack confidence in our appearance. And if we do not think that we are important enough to do what it takes to improve what causes us to feel inferior, we will continue to settle for less than God's best.

Over the past few decades obesity in women has increased at an alarming rate. Lack of exercise and a regular diet of fast food have taken its toll on us. Sadly obesity not only affects our appearance but also our health. There has been a drastic increase in the diagnoses of hypertension and diabetes in women of all ages. Shopping in the plus sized department is no longer limited to the over forty crowd, but often includes women under twenty years old. Whether we are battling a weight problem or other issues that cause us to tend to settle for less than we know that we deserve, we must realize that we are the workmanship of God and precious to him. Our very lives are a gift from him, and we must learn to love ourselves unconditionally, even with the weight problem, hair that won't grow, problem skin, or other things that we dislike about our appearance.

Begin to look at yourself the way that God looks at you. The Word of God says, "I will praise thee; for I am fearfully and wonderfully made: marvelous are thy works; and that my soul knoweth right well" (Psalm 139: 14 [KJV]). As a child of God you know that it is impossible for God to lie; therefore, his word is always true. We are God's workmanship, and the psalmist declares that his works are "marvelous." Let's take a look at the word marvelous for a moment. Marvelous is defined as, "of the highest kind or quality, notably superior," not inferior, or lacking quality or class but *the best*. How dare we think ourselves unworthy of the best God has for us, when his Word proclaims that we are "marvelous."

The psalmist said, "I will praise thee," Psalm 139; 14 (KJV) so let praise be your first step in receiving what God's Word says about you. Go ahead and give God some praise right now!! Just begin to bless His name, because you are precious in his sight girlfriend!! He adores you, he sent his only Son to die for you!! You may not be a size eight, but God says you're of "high quality," You may have molested, abused, cheated on, or promiscuous, but your Daddy says, you are "notably superior." After all, it's not what your parents said, your critics, or your so-called friends said; it's what *God* says about you that counts. Jesus Christ our

Lord and Savior came down from his throne, took on an earthly body, was ridiculed, mocked, called a devil, and was then put to death in the most horrifying manner known on this earth just for you. He didn't have to do it, but he did it anyway. He loved you so much that he offered his own life in order to save yours. How dare you believe that you are not worthy of love and the best that God has to offer! You must learn to love yourself unconditionally, as God does. In doing so you will reflect an inward confidence and an outward glow that will cause you to attract what God desires for you, *his best.*

Having the ability to love yourself not only raises your self-esteem but also helps you to change the things that you feel are essential to improving your health, appearance and emotional well-being. If we eat unhealthy foods every day, and fail to exercise, we do not love ourselves because we are not honoring our temple. The Bible says:

What? No ye not that your body is the temple of the Holy Ghost, which is in you, which ye have of God, and that ye are not your own? For ye are bought with a price, therefore glorify God in your body and in your spirit which are God's.

I Corinthians 6:19-20 (KJV)

Jesus paid a dear price for our salvation and our physical health;

so we are obligated to honor his sacrifice by living holy and caring for our bodies. Christians love to quote Isaiah 53:5 (KJV) "But he was wounded for our transgressions, he was bruised for our iniquities, the chastisement of our peace was upon him, and with his stripes we are healed," However, most of us fail to realize that we have an important role to play in maintaining our good health. Failing to honor our temple is blatant disobedience to the Father, therefore, it is sin.

For every spiritual action there is an opposite sinful reaction. God says honor your temple and the world says "be comfortable in the skin you're in. Well the devil is a liar, if the skin you're in can shorten your life; then you need to become very uncomfortable in it. It is unrealistic to believe that we will all be thin; as some of us have always been, and will always be full-figured. But developing healthy eating habits and exercising a few days a week are doable for most of us. Begin by walking thirty minutes a day or riding a stationary bicycle for twenty minutes four times a week in order to build endurance. The devil wants us to die young, because as long as we live, we remain a threat to him. Why give him what he wants? He is **not** your friend. He wants to **kill** you, he is your enemy! The Bible says, "The thief cometh not, but for to steal, and to kill, and to destroy: I am come that they might have life, and that they might have it more abundantly" (John 10:10, [KJV]). Whom do you serve the thief or the Lord? If you are living for the Lord then you must *submit* to his word and honor your temple.

I beseech you therefore, brethren, by the mercies of God, that ye present your bodies a living sacrifice, holy, acceptable, unto God, which is your reasonable service. And be not conformed to this world; but be ye transformed by the renewing of your mind, that ye may prove what is that good, and acceptable and perfect will of God.

Romans 12:1-2 (KJV)

Make small changes that help you to look and feel better. Increase your intake of fruits and vegetables, and drink at least eight glasses of water daily, limit sweets and starches and eliminate white flour, rice, breads, white potatoes and pasta from your diet. Whole wheat pasta, bread and brown rice, and sweet potatoes, or yams are much healthier. Take a picture of yourself, post it along with a picture of an item of clothing you would like to be able to wear on your refrigerator. Every time you lose fifteen pounds take another picture of yourself and replace the first with it. You see, everything in this life requires that we go through a process, even weight loss. Remember to give God the glory when you complete a workout or stick to your healthy eating plan all day.

Truly loving yourself means taking the time to care for your own needs as well as the needs of others. We must learn to spend quality time just pampering ourselves. Due to the current economic conditions the unemployment rate has been on the rise for some time. For those of us who are no longer employed or are trying to cut expenses in order to stash emergency funds in the event of layoffs in our companies, take heart; we can pamper ourselves without going over our budgets. If you are one of those ladies who can no longer afford to go to the nail or hair salon, or day spa, or if you have decided that your money is better spent elsewhere you can pamper yourself at home for less than half the cost.

As daughters of the Most High God we should reflect who we are at all times. Our hair and clothing should be neat and our nails at least clean and shaped. Going to the salon is not an option for some of us currently; therefore, it is necessary to either learn to care for our own hair or to employ the help of a friend who is more skilled. Many salon quality hair care products can be purchased at beauty supply stores or department stores. Remember that less is more, and opt for low maintenance styles if you are financially challenged. Check out the Internet for free hair care and styling instructions. If at all possible have your hair trimmed professionally every six weeks. Keep your hair tight, you never know when God will send Mr. Right!

Wearing nail polish or acrylic nails is a matter of personal taste. Some of us desire to make a fashion statement with our nails, and others just want neat, clean, well kept, unpolished nails. Whatever your preference, please keep your nails clean and shaped. Believe it or not people notice how your hands look. Dirty, broken or bitten nails give a negative impression of the type of woman that you are. If your job requires you to perform tasks that cause your nails to get dirty, clean them as soon as you get home each day to keep the dirt from getting imbedded underneath your nails. Men notice your hands, especially if they are interested in getting to know you, because they are usually checking the left one out to see if there is a wedding band or engagement ring on your finger. It is equally important that you take care of your feet. Remember that they take you everywhere that you go, and neglecting them can cause serious problems. You don't have to spend thirty of forty dollars on a pedicure to have healthy, beautiful feet. There are enough do-it-yourself products on the market that you can do your pedicures at home.

Remember that this is about learning to love yourself, and building your self-esteem. Make changes that you can live with for the rest of your life. Do not begin a beauty regime that you do not plan to continue once you are married. Women often complain that their husbands change after they've been married for some time. One of the most common complaints is that the compliments stop. But could *we* be part of the problem? Some of us are guilty of *false advertising* before marriage. During the honeymoon phase we go to the beauty shop and nail salon every week, and wear the beautiful lingerie to bed every night. Somewhere along the line we become so comfortable that we pull the hair back in a pony tail; stop the nail appointments and don the granny sleepwear. Men do not like change. If a man falls in love with you believing that you are a sensual and fashionable lady, and then discovers that everything that he believed you to be is a lie, there will be trouble in paradise. If you fake it you will not make it!

Taking pride in your appearance also requires that we dress in clothing that suits our body types. Whether plus-sized or petite we can look good if we choose the right garments. Be sure to wear clothing that is the correct size. Do not wear clothing that is too tight or several sizes too large for you. Sometimes full-figured women tend to wear clothing that is too large in order to "hide" unattractive bulges and bumps. However, this only makes us look larger which defeats the purpose. Wearing clothing too tight is not attractive on a lady of any size, nor does it reflect godliness. And ladies, men know that we have breasts; so there is no need for us to display them. We don't need to advertise anything that is not available on the open market, however, dressing tastefully in stylish clothing shows that we are well kept women of God.

The first thing people notice about you is your face; therefore, taking care of your skin should be high priority in your daily regime. No matter how beautiful you are, if your skin is not properly cared for it may age prematurely, or cause you to develop dry patches or other blemishes on your face. Some of us have been misled in the belief that our ethnicity alone prevents aging skin, however, with increased pollution due to greenhouse gases and other pollutants it has become necessary to rely on more than our heritage to prevent aging or damaged skin. When hearing the word skincare some of us automatically think of makeup such as foundations, eye shadows, liners and other products. The fact is that skincare is not about applying makeup; it is about properly cleansing and moisturizing the skin. Makeup is a glamour product and when applied to unhealthy skin it merely covers up the problem; while properly selected skincare products help to correct or minimize the problem. Have you ever seen a lady with a thick layer of makeup over blemished skin? It actually magnifies the problem, as being over made-up draws more attention to the blemishes. As most of us are short on time and or money, it is possible to adopt a simple skin care regime that takes only about five minutes morning and night. Cleansing and moisturizing the skin with the products suited to your skin type or as recommended by your dermatologist or skin care professional can help to alleviate dryness, blemishes and oiliness. Sacrificing a few minutes morning and night and a few dollars a month to pamper your skin is well worth the increased confidence and compliments that you will receive. Like sin, unhealthy skin cannot be covered up for long!

Loving ourselves means taking the time to build our self-esteem, improve our health, and spend time pampering ourselves. As women we often give so much of our time to our loved ones that we *lose* ourselves. Learning to love yourself before entering into marriage will make you a more confident and well rounded person. Creating good eating and exercise habits, taking the time to care for your hair and skin are simple luxuries that we *can* afford with a little creativity. God only gives us one body, and we must take the time to care for it.

Father in the Name of Jesus, I ask that you forgive me for neglecting my temple. Your word says, "Whether therefore ye eat, or drink, or whatsoever you do, do all to the glory of God" (I Corinthians, 10:31 [KJV]). From this day forward, I commit to following a healthy lifestyle, so that I might live the long healthy life that you desire for me, in Jesus Name, Amen

Four
Submit To God

Humble yourselves therefore under the mighty hand of
God that he may exalt you in due time.
I Peter 5:6 (KJV)

Today's woman is well educated, independent, and often earns much higher salaries than their male counterparts. We are authors, pastors, bishops, college professors, doctors, lawyers and CEO's of our own companies. We have come a long way since the days of not having the right to vote, or to go to college. Society has for the most part, accepted women as equals in regard to careers. This is indeed cause for celebration, and we should be thankful to God for the opportunities afforded to us today. However, some of us have allowed our independence to cause us to view *submission* as negative behavior. The world teaches us that if we are educated and financially stable we are self-sufficient. However, as Christian women we must realize that we are forever dependent on God and are required to submit to him and obey his Word. This means that we are to obey his commandments and walk in his precepts.

Our first act of submission to God, is when we accept the Lord Jesus Christ as our Savior. By confessing our sins and asking forgiveness for them we are submitting to God and renouncing our sinful lifestyles. We then enter into relationship with our Lord and Savior and receive the gift of eternal life and the blessings of Abraham upon our lives. We become joint heirs with Jesus Christ. Since heaven is his eternal home, it is ours as well. We even have the same Father. Glory to God!! Submission to God does not take anything away from us, but adds more to our lives then we could have ever imagined.

The bible proclaims, "Know ye that the Lord he is God: it is he that made us, and not we ourselves: we are his people and the sheep of his pasture" (Psalm 100:3 [KJV]). We were created by God, and as his people we are commanded to submit to him. Submit means, "To yield to governance or authority." We are God's creation, and if we are saved we are his sheep. If we know anything about the relationship between a shepherd and his sheep, then we know that the *shepherd leads* the herd. The sheep do not ask the shepherd why he is taking them in a certain direction; or why they have to graze in a particular field, or when they are going to be sheared. They simply follow the shepherd as he is responsible for their well-being. When the sheep stray from the flock, they put themselves in danger. The 23rd Psalm (KJV) says, "The Lord is my shepherd, I shall not want." When we submit to the Lord and follow him, we discover that he provides us with his protection and meets our every need. But when we stray from the shepherd's protection; the cost can be higher than we desire to pay.

Once we learn to submit to God, we will find it easier to submit to every part of his Word. Yes, even the scripture that states, "Wives submit yourselves to your own husbands as unto the Lord" (Ephesians 5:22 [KJV]). Have you ever noticed how many married Christian ladies begin to squirm in their pews when the preacher reads this verse? Isn't it amazing how many amens, and hallelujahs the pastor gets until then? It seems that either their love thermometer is malfunctioning or the Word has convicted them. Like it or not, the Word of God commands us to submit to our husbands which means to yield to their authority. The word is speaking about Godly husbands, men who love the Lord and walk in obedience to him; those who love their wives as Christ loves the church. God does not command us to submit to our husbands because he feels we are less important, but because he has called the man to be the head of the family. As the stronger vessel he is to bear the responsibilities of the household, and we are to support him and encourage him. We are not to become victims of abuse, or lose our self-esteem. We are to be loved, cherished, protected and covered by a godly husband spiritually, physically and financially. We are to honor our husbands by talking with him before making major decisions that affect the household, by building him up to others and not belittling him, and by avoiding any behavior that would embarrass him publicly. The word of God says of the virtuous woman, "The heart of her husband doth safely trust in her, so that he shall have no need of spoil. She will do him good and not evil all the days of her life "(Proverbs 31: 11-12 [KJV]). Are you a virtuous woman? Have you truly submitted to God in every area of your life?

When asking God to send you a husband who will love you the way God has commanded him to, remember that God also requires us to love, honor and *obey* our husbands. This statement is often altered in the wedding vows; and a more modern version is adopted. However, as a woman of God you are not to adapt to the ways of the world. If you are confident enough that the man you plan to marry is sent by God; then why do you need the word obey excluded from your wedding vows? Why would you object to the preacher pronouncing you man and wife, and not husband and wife? Do you consider the word *wife* offensive? If so, why have you prayed so long to become one? Be honest with yourself and your potential mate about how you feel. You may discover that you need to remain single until you have matured enough spiritually to submit to a godly husband.

Father in the Name of Jesus, I confess that I struggle with submitting my will and my way to you. I desire to become a woman of virtue, so that both you and my future mate can trust me to do good and not evil all the days of my life, in Jesus' name, Amen

Five
Care For Your Home

She sets about her work vigorously; her arms are strong
for her task.
Proverbs 31:17 (NIV)

While it is true that men are attracted to a pretty face, they also pay attention to a woman's home when they enter. Pay very close attention the next time a gentleman enters your home for the first time; his eyes will take in the entire room. He may comment that you have a nice place, or merely smile and say nothing. He is probably not assessing the price of your furniture or your wall art; it is more likely that he is analyzing your personality, style and ability to maintain order in your home. The following are simple tips to creating and maintaining a well-kept and orderly home that gives you the confidence to open the door without hesitation, even to unexpected guests.

Organization is the key to good housekeeping. When everything is in its proper place maintaining order and cleanliness is much easier. The first step to creating a well-kept home is to de-clutter. Do not treasure your trash! For some reason we often find it difficult to discard things we no longer use; which cause our homes to become filled

with clutter. Clutter not only prevents us from keeping our home orderly, but also takes up space that is needed for new or useful things. Closets, dressers, desks, bathroom and kitchen cabinets, refrigerators, freezers and laundry rooms are the most common sites for clutter. Along with causing disorder in your home, clutter can also increase household expenses. For example, if your kitchen cabinets are so cluttered that you do not know that you already have 4 cans of the same vegetable, you will probably spend money at the supermarket buying more. Or your broom closet may have several bottles of the same all-purpose cleaner if it is not organized. Stop wasting your hard earned money and get your home in order.

Begin to de-clutter your home by organizing it one room at the time. Remember that it took more than one day for your home to get into the cluttered state that it is in, and it will take more than one day to get it organized. When going through your closets make three stacks;

keep, give (or sell), and throw away. Next, don't fool yourself; if you can't remember when you have used or worn and item; either give it charity, have a yard sale, or throw it away. When coming across books and other items that you borrowed from family or friends, but failed to return, apologize and give them back! Finally, prevent future clutter by going through closets, dressers etc at least once every two months. Refusing to remove clutter from your home indicates fear of change and disregard for order! God loves order and we are supposed to love what he loves.

As godly women we should *keep* our homes clean. Working five days a week; cleaning, doing laundry and running errands on Saturday, and then attending church on Sunday can seem overwhelming. However, with a little "strategic planning" it is possible to achieve weekly goals, without becoming physically and spiritually drained. By spreading out house cleaning chores throughout the week, cleaning all day on Saturday can be avoided. If you have children be sure to assign chores to them and *do not* let them off the hook!

The kitchen and bathroom tend to require more frequent cleaning than other areas of the house, therefore, cleaning them in the middle of the week, make Saturday's "touch up" a breeze. While dinner is simmering on Wednesday evening, tackle the bathroom cleaning. After dinner, (since you have to wash your dishes anyway) wipe down your countertops, sink, refrigerator and stove top, and clean the floor. Getting up thirty minutes earlier and running the vacuum before going to work on Friday is also a time-saver. While chatting on the phone with girlfriend, whip out the duster and clean the coffee tables, etc. Just taking the time to do a little bit during the week, can free up most of your Saturdays. Couldn't you use more time to relax or pamper yourself on the weekend?

If you have not already done so, take the time to make your home attractive. You do not have to spend a lot of money to add your personal touch to each room of your house. Check out local garage sales, and flea markets. You can often find wall hangings, mirrors, and decorative picture frames at bargain prices. Place live or artificial green plants on tables, or on plant stands to add a touch of elegance to any room. Put your heart into your home. Proverbs 31:22 (KJV) says of the virtuous woman, "She maketh herself coverings of tapestry; her clothing is silk and purple." The virtuous woman takes care with the appearance of both her home and herself. Make your home a well organized, tastefully decorated haven; that reflects the virtuous woman that you really are.

Father in the name of Jesus, I ask that you forgive me for neglecting to care for the home that you have blessed me with. Give me the strength to de-clutter, and to maintain order n my household, in Jesus name, Amen.

Six
Be A Good Steward

And by knowledge shall the chambers be filled with all
precious and pleasant riches.
Proverbs 24:4 (KJV)

The nation's current economic condition has caused many of us to take a closer look at our finances; particularly in the areas of earning and spending money. With Fortune 500 companies, closing, merging with other corporations and filing for bankruptcy, many of us have found ourselves facing serious financial crises. The Word of God tells us that the Lord is "Jehovah-Jireh (The Lord our Provider), and, "But my God shall supply all your need according to his riches in glory by Christ Jesus" (Philippians 4:19 [KJV]). As single Christian women most of us have experienced God's divine provision at some point in our lives. We know that he is, "Able to do exceedingly abundantly above all that we ask or think, according to the power that worketh in us" (Ephesians 3:20 [KJV]). Praise God for his divine provision! Praise him for making a way out of no way! Praise him for his grace and his mercy! He is constant in his love, and his compassion toward us, yet he expects us to learn from our experiences so that we remain prosperous.

Over the past year the unemployment rate has continued to rise. Many hardworking Americans have gone to bed employed; only to get up the next morning and find that they have joined the ranks of the unemployed. It is impossible for us to predict or control the actions of anyone other than our own; however, careful planning can help us to be better prepared in the event of corporate down-sizing. Following the principles set in the Word of God; and seeking his direction in the choices that we make in regard to saving, and spending the money that we earn is essential to avoiding financial devastation. God has promised to bless us if we obey him in our giving. Let's reflect on his promise:

Bring ye all the tithes into the storehouse, that there may be meat in mine house, and prove me now herewith, saith the Lord of hosts, if I will not open up the windows of heaven, and pour you out a blessing, that there shall not be room enough to receive it.

Malachi 3:10 (KJV)

We know that God always keeps his Word, to us. However, when he pours out financial blessings on us, we must learn how to manage the overflow. If we spend our inheritance without considering the consequences, we will end up like the prodigal son in the Gospel of Luke Chapter 15. This parable has been taught by countless men and women of God with a focus on the Father's willingness to forgive us when we sin against him. There is great comfort in the knowledge that God is waiting with open arms when we leave the "hog pen" of sin and return to him. However, this parable also warns us of the consequences of reckless spending. What most Christians fail to understand is that *all* money belongs to God, not only the tithe; and just because we give the tenth it does not give us the right to squander the ninety percent that we are allowed to keep. Yes, we work for the wages, but when we find ourselves in financial trouble it is God that we ask for help. The Word of God says, "All things were made by him, and without him was not any thing made that was made"(John 1:3 [KJV]). Neither our jobs nor money would exist without God. He is the one that gives us favor with the company when we are seeking employment, and he is the one that gives us the wisdom to perform the work. Therefore, we need to honor him by being good stewards of the ninety percent that we keep.

Providing all of the financial support for the home on one salary can be difficult; and saving money for retirement, emergencies, or vacations seems nearly impossible. But there are several ways to save money and build a small nest egg over time. For example, if you eat out for lunch everyday, stop!! Bring yourself a healthy lunch from home and treat yourself by dining out for lunch or dinner once a month. If you purchase groceries for your home, and then eat out at lunch everyday, you are actually buying groceries *twice*. We make poor choices like this, and then wonder why we are not able to save money.

If you spend $5 a day eating out at lunch; it cost you $25 per week, $100 per month, which adds up to $1200 per year. You could have deposited that money into a savings account and earned interest on it. Remember the servant in the gospel of Matthew Chapter 25, who buried his talent and when the master returned his talent was taken from him and given to the servant that had ten talents? Jesus expects us to earn interest on the money that he allows us to earn. When we are wasteful we prevent God from blessing us in the way that he desires. We must prove our faithfulness over what we have in order to be equipped to handle the overflow.

As little girls we dreamed of the day our prince will come and take and to the beautiful castle on the hill. We had visions of drinking from golden goblets, and being draped in the finest attire. We had maidservants and menservants, and we lived happily ever after, with an endless supply of money and all of the other things that our hearts desire. In our fantasy world there are no electric bills, utilities or car payments; because our prince was ruler of the entire kingdom. Wake up! We are not little girls any longer, nor are we fairy princesses living in a castle; and if we don't learn to become good stewards of our money, it will run out!

As Christian women, we know the consequences of living as if there is no tomorrow. When we were in sin, we partied, and committed other atrocities against God as if we would live forever, and as if there was no hell for us to go to. Now that we are children of God we should consider the consequences before we act, even when it comes to our finances. The Bible says "And be ye not conformed to this world; but be ye transformed by the renewing of your mind, that ye may prove what is that good and acceptable and perfect will of God" (Romans 12:2 [KJV]). The world encourages us to spend because we *deserve* to; but God tells us to be good stewards of our money. Who are we going to listen to? Some of us have not been blessed in our finances because God knows we are just going to waste the overflow anyway! Learn how to save some of the money that you work so hard to earn. Try saving at least $1 each day, by the end of the year you will have at least $365 in the bank. It may not seem like much, but something saved is better than nothing saved!

We must also learn how to prepare our households. The next time you shop pay attention to the way that men purchase items in grocery or discount stores. Most of them tend to buy large packages of goods, items in bulk, or several packages of the same product. There are two main reasons for their shopping technique; first, most of them don't like to shop, second, they don't like to run out of the things that they use every day. Keeping a home stocked with every day items is one of the principles of the Proverbs 31 woman. The bible proclaims that, "When it snows, she has no fear for her household; for all of them are clothed in scarlet" (Proverbs 31:21 [NIV]). This means that when the "season changes" she is not worried about her family lacking provisions, because she has prepared her household in advance. We do not have to hoard goods, in order to prepare our household but we do need to prepare for the unexpected.

Go to the ant, you sluggard; consider its ways and be wise! It has no commander, no overseer or ruler.

Yet is stores its provision in summer, and gathers its food at harvest. How long will you lie there, you sluggard? When will you get up from your sleep? A little sleep, a little slumber a little folding of the hands to rest, and poverty shall come upon you like a bandit and scarcity like an armed man.

Proverbs 6:6-11 ((NIV)

We were created in the image and likeness of God; so how can the ant know better how to prepare its household than we do? God expects us to store goods for our households. In the winter months we face high heating costs, rising prices in food, gasoline, and other goods. Although we cannot control higher prices, we can reduce future costs by stocking up on dry goods, paper products, and canned goods during the summer and fall. The virtuous woman planned ahead; therefore, when winter came she was not concerned. Winter does not always represent temperature change, but sometimes refers to the hard times; such as a reduction in hours at the workplace, lay-offs, sickness, or skyrocketing prices. Have you prepared your household for winter? Is your pantry well stocked enough to sustain you in the event that you were out of work for six months? Remember that the man that you are asking God to send into your life is expecting you to be more than a pretty face and an hourglass figure. Some of you have asked the Lord to send you wealthy husbands that will love and take good care of you. However, if you can't manage your own money, or prepare your household as a single Christian woman, you will not suddenly receive an *anointing* to manage the household or the budget when you marry. Get your financial house in order, so that you can *add* and not just *take* from the marriage. Your husband should be confident that like the virtuous woman; the choices that you make will benefit the household. So buying clothing and other items and then hiding them in the trunk of your car, until you can slip them past your husband, is unacceptable. This is deception, and all deception is of the devil!

Father, in the name of Jesus, I ask that you give me the wisdom that I need to manage my finances. I ask that you forgive me for taking the finances that you have blessed me with for granted. From this day forward I will think before I spend, and I will begin to prepare my home for winter. I will no longer allow the ant's home to be more prepared than mine. I realize that I must learn to manage my own finances, before I will be able to manage the household of myself and my future mate. Help me to make wise choices that will build my home and not tear it down, in Jesus name, Amen.

Seven
Avenues Of Income

In her hand she holds he distaff, and grasps the spindle
with her fingers.
Proverbs 31:19 (NIV)

It is indeed a blessing to be gainfully employed, and to enjoy all of the perks our corporations offer such as retirement plans, life and health insurance, paid vacations and holidays and stock options. However, during the country's recent financial crisis many of us have found ourselves out of work, and relying on unemployment compensation to provide us with the bare necessities.

The bible says of the virtuous women, "She considers a field and buys it; and out of her earnings she plants a vineyard" (Proverbs 31: 16 [NIV]). The virtuous woman is a *business* woman. The bible also says of her, "She makes linen garments and sells them, and supplies the merchants with sashes" (Proverbs 31: 24 [NIV]). Not only is the virtuous woman a business woman; but she has *multiple* avenues of income. She does not rely on *the company* for her family's needs. That is why she does not worry about her household in winter; she has money coming in from *multiple* directions.

The most common excuse for failing to have multiple avenues of income is, "I just don't have time." Well, do you have time for your electricity to be turned off, or your car repossessed because you've lost your job and have no other income?" Or would you rather *make* the time to research additional earnings opportunities, so that *your house* will be covered in winter? Remember, that winter not only refers to the temperature in a given season, but also to difficult situations in life. In these modern times we have a wealth of conveniences that the Proverbs 31, (virtuous woman) could never have imagined. We have cars, microwave ovens, computers, the Internet, washers and dryers, electric and gas ranges, and a host of other conveniences, yet we have the nerve to say that we do not have *time* to do more.

Can you imagine preparing meals over an open fire, or washing clothes in the river, or even walking everywhere that you go? The virtuous woman ran her household successfully in a primitive environment, yet had the *time* to run several businesses. The virtuous woman is not talking on the phone for two hours with girlfriend; nor is she surfing the Internet while she could be *earning money* on it! The word of God says that, "She watches over the affairs of her household and does not eat the bread of idleness" (Proverbs 31:287 [NIV]). Yes, taking the time to relax and unwind is beneficial for our spiritual, physical, and mental health, but making sure that our households are covered is equally important.

Creating an additional avenue of income can be as simple as doing something that you love, and getting paid for it. For example, if you are good at altering clothing, why not turn your gift into a business. If you enjoy baking, take a cake decorating class that specializes in baking birthday cakes for children. Then turn your newly learned skill into extra income, by baking and selling birthday cakes for the children of your friends, family, neighbors and members of your congregation. Do you play the piano or organ at your local church? If so, run a small advertisement in your local newspaper, offering to play for weddings, revivals, or other Christian events. Do you love planning events such as dinner parties, weddings, or other social gatherings? If you are in your element when arranging these social affairs, then consider becoming and event planner.

God has given each of his children unique gifts and talents; and there is *no* reason for us to live in poverty and lack. There are no limits on what we can achieve as long as we walk upright before the Lord, and give *him* the praise and glory for our successes! God's word does tell us that we are supposed to work, but God never intended for his people to rely on the world's system for their prosperity. The bible tells us that, "For even when we were with you, this we commanded you, that if any would not work, neither should he eat" (2 Thessalonians 3:10 [KJV]).

As single Christian women, we are the only bread-winners in our homes. Our jobs are designed to supply our basic needs; such as shelter, transportation, food, clothing and utilities. However, if we desire to become prosperous we must use the gifts and talents that God has given us. How many people do you know that have become prosperous working their normal 9 to 5? Thank God for the 9 to 5's, they keep us from living on the streets, and freezing or starving to death. God bless our employers for providing health insurance, life insurance and all of the other benefits that we enjoy. But what happens when the company decides that they have to reduce staff, just to keep the company afloat? What happens when sales drop, clients don't renew their contracts or the firm files for bankruptcy? The paycheck stops. So let us be, "wise as servants and harmless as doves," (Matthew 10:16 [KJV]) so that we are able to survive when or if the firm fails. We are responsible for making sure that our households are covered, not our employers. Be wise like the virtuous woman, and prepare in the summer so that you do not have to worry in the winter. The virtuous woman does face trouble but she is prepared; therefore she has nothing to fear. The bible says, "She is clothed with strength and dignity; she can laugh at the days to come" (Proverbs 31:25 [NIV]). The virtuous woman is so confident that her household is prepared, that in the midst of famine, lay-off, and corporate down-sizing she laughs! She knows that there is food in the pantry, money in the bank, and that even more money is coming to her from her businesses! How about you?

Father in the name of Jesus, I confess that I failed to use the gifts and talents that you have blessed me with so liberally. You gave me these gifts to not only to bless others, but for me to blessed as well. You never intended for your children to lead mediocre lives, but to be prosperous financially, spiritually and physically. Forgive me for allowing my gifts and talents to stagnate. From today forward, I will stir up the gifts within me, in the name of Jesus, Amen.

Eight
Wait To Be Found

And Jacob served seven years for Rachel, and they
seemed unto him but a few days, for the love he had
to her.
Genesis 29:20 (KJV)

As Christian women we desire God's best sons, and are drawn to those who are most gifted and anointed. It has even been said that some of our sisters have literally *chased* men of God at Christian events. By the way, do you realize that if you have to chase a man to get his attention, he doesn't really want you? And as soon as he finds someone he does want, he is going to drop you like a hot skillet! The world tells us that it's okay for the *liberated* woman to make the first move, if she meets a man that piques her interest. However, as women of God, we know that the bible tells us, "Whoso findeth a wife findeth a good thing, and obtaineth favor of the Lord "(Proverbs 18:22 [KJV]). God's word clearly tells us that the man is supposed to find the wife, not the reverse. God has not changed his mind! We are to be ladies in waiting, not women on the prowl. Godly men are looking for ladies, and real ladies do not chase men no matter how liberated they are. If a man is interested in meeting you, he will not allow anything or anyone to stand in his way. And if he really wants to make you his lady, he will do whatever is necessary to win your heart.

When we go after a man, we are not only behaving inappropriately, but we are guilty of rebelling against God. There is nothing *liberating* about chasing a man, unless he has snatched your purse! Spend time seeking God, get to know him intimately and he will send you the man your heart desires. God is all-knowing and he does not need you to fill out a questionnaire for him in order to select the mate that he has designed for you. He does not make mistakes, mismatches or *think* the two of you *might* hit if off! The bible says, "Except the Lord builds the house, they labor in vain that build it; except the Lord keep the city, the watchman waketh but in vain" (Psalm 127:1 [KJV]). Do you desire a lasting marriage, or a temporary solution for loneliness? If you want the kind of marital relationship that God desires for us, put your trust in him. He is the *Master* builder. He knows all about you and your potential mate, because he created both of you. God knows who you will be able to love and commit to for the rest of your life, and who you would leave in a heartbeat if they just rub you the wrong way once too often. Some of us have been married and divorced before we were saved, but now that we are women of God we must realize that God does not take the marital vows lightly, and expects our marriages to last a lifetime. The bible says that, "Ye are the light of the world. A city that is set on a hill cannot be hid" (Matthew 5:14 [KJV]). That means that we are to be examples to the world, and should never behave like the ungodly. Being like a city on a hill means that we are in clear view; the world sees everything that we do.

The possibility of marrying a pastor or bishop seems to excite most Christian women, and some of us are living in the *First Lady Fantasy*. However, it takes a special lady to walk in this calling. The word lady is defined as, "A woman of refinement and *gentle* manners." To be refined means to be, "free of impurities." First is defined as, "having the highest or most prominent part among a group of similar voices or instruments." To have the prominent part means that you are, "readily noticeable." First Ladies stand out; and everything that they do or say is scrutinized. The way that they dress, keep their homes, and nurture their families is critiqued by members of their congregation as well as their community. This position of honor requires discipline, patience, longsuffering, and the gift of forgiveness. Has God called you to be a *First Lady?* Are you free from impurities? Do you have a pure heart? Does your personality reflect gentleness to others? Are you an example to women on your job, in your community, and in your church? How well do you handle scrutiny, persecution and criticism? If you are living in the *First Lady Fantasy* let it go! If God has shown you that your future mate is a pastor or leader, then ask him to mold you into the refined, gentle lady that he requires you to be. The word of God says, "As a prisoner of the Lord, then, I urge you to live a life worthy of the calling you have received "(Ephesians 4:1 [NIV]). As children of God we know that he will give us the ability to complete our assignments on this earth. The Bible says, "Being confident of this that he who began a good work in you will carry it on to completion until the day of Christ Jesus" (Philippians 1:6 [NIV]). But whatever you do, never chase a man; if he likes you and you like him, just run slowly enough for him to catch *you*!

Father in the name of Jesus, I ask that you mold me into the refined and gentle lady that I need to be. I renounce the advice that the world gives about seeking a mate; and receive what your word says in that it is the man that finds the wife, in Jesus name. Amen.

Nine
Refuse To Settle

And the King loved Esther above all the women, and
she obtained grace and favor in his sight more than all
of the virgins, so that he set the royal crown upon her
head and made her queen instead of Vashti.
Esther 2:17 (KJV)

Now that we have prepared ourselves for our future mates
from the inside out, the final step is to wait for God to
send them to us. While waiting for your mate it is more
important now than ever to, "Watch and pray that ye enter not into
temptation; the spirit indeed is willing but the flesh is weak" (Matthew
26:41 [KJV]). God is not the only one that has been watching your
progress; so has the enemy. He knows that you have been seeking God's
will for your life, and that you have been spending quality time with
the Lord. He also knows that you have gotten your household and

your finances in order, and that you have dropped a couple of pounds. He realizes that you are more confident in your God and yourself than you have ever been in your life. You have become a well-rounded single Christian woman, to whom prayer has become as natural as breathing, and he is *angry*. He is just waiting for you to fall into the same dysfunctional relationships that you have in the past. Don't give him what he wants!

As women of God we have to be aware of the devil's devices. He is constantly wandering the earth, setting traps for the children of God. He cannot create; so everything that comes from him is counterfeit. We must understand that some of us may encounter an "imposter" before the mate that God has for us comes on the scene, therefore, we cannot become lax in our prayer lives. Don't you feel that your time is much too valuable to waste on a counterfeit mate? The counterfeit mate can only imitate the real thing, so keep your spiritual eyes open. It does not matter if a cat can bark like a dog; it is still a cat!

The bible clearly tells us, "Be ye not unequally yoked together with unbelievers; for what fellowship has righteousness with unrighteousness, and what communion has light with darkness?" (II Corinthians 6:14 [KJV]). *Do not* date unsaved men, no matter how nice you think they are, or who introduces them to you! Please remember that just because he goes to church, that does not mean he is saved. If you believe in living holy and he believes its okay to party all night on Saturday and then go to church and sit on the deacon board or in the pulpit on Sunday; then God did not send this man to you. If he is still living with his mother, grandmother or some other relative because he can't afford to live in his own place; run! If he cannot keep a job, a vehicle, or is financially unstable; run! You have worked too hard to get yourself prepared from the inside out for your mate. God *will not* send one of his daughters "a piece of man." He will send you his best and only his best, anything else is of the devil! God called the man to be the head of the house and of the wife; how can he head something that he cannot support? The king put the crown on Esther and made her queen, not vice versa. Boaz had his workers drop handfuls on purpose for Ruth (Ruth 2:17); not the other way around. Keep your money in your pocket, if you can buy the man, so can someone else!

When you first began to pray to the Father for a mate, you were very specific about the type of mate that you desired. God does not have a memory problem; he is all-knowing and Almighty. He cannot get Alzheimer's or amnesia; therefore, he remembers every word spoken to him in prayer. So when he sends your mate, he will be the one that your heart desires. He will not need to be fixed, changed or mothered. He will be the husband that God has commanded him to be, and that you need for him to be. He will love you the way that Christ loved the church, and he will cover you in the ways that a godly husband is required to. The word of God says, "If a son ask bread of any of you that is a father, will he give him a stone? Or if he ask a fish, will he for a fish give him a serpent?" (Luke 11:11 [KJV]). We know that no godly parent would give their child anything that is inferior or harmful to them. Therefore, we can trust our Heavenly Father to give us his best sons. Do not settle for less than the Father desires for you, and do not settle for less than you prayed for. Watch and pray daily, so that you will be able to avoid the enemy's trap. Trust in the Lord, and *wait* for your mate.

Notes

Chapter One

1. http://www.merriam-webster.com/dictionary/meditate

2. http://www.merriam-webster.com/dictionary/trust

Chapter Three

1. http://www.merriam-webster.com/dictionary/marvelous

Chapter Eight

1. http://www.merriam-webster.com/dictionary/lady

2. http://www.merriam-webster.com/dictionary/first

3. http://www.merriam-webster.com/dictionary/refined

4. http://www.merriam-webster.com/dictionary/prominent